An Awful Lot

a collection of original poetry

WILLIAM SICKWITT

An Awful Lot
By William Sickwitt

Copyright © 2013 by Michele Baker

Cover photograph by William Sickwitt
Illustrations and design by Nicole Bless, nicolebless.com

Special thanks to William Hayes for his review and insight. Also to Andrew Dumas who edited the Biography and Dianne Zavatsky who edited the poems.

ALL RIGHTS RESERVED. This book contains material protected under International and Federal Copyright Laws and Treaties. Any unauthorized reprint or use of this material is prohibited. No part of this book may be reproduced or transmitted in any form or by any means, electronic or mechanical, including photocopying, recording, or by any information storage and retrieval system without express written permission from the author/publisher.

tall and slim with a crooked grin

hazel eyes with a twinkle of mischief

that's how I would describe the man Sickwitt

Until we meet again.

Your loving sister,

Michele

Here's to my ex-wife

Here's to me

Here's to spilling some humor

On the family tree

· · · · · · · · ·

contents

Preface: Good Books & Speak Well	1
Chapter 1: An Awful Lot of Tree	**3**
Boob	4
Loki	5
Luna	5
Huff	6
AppleWho?	7
Loved by One at Least	7
Change	8
Talking Bout Money	8
Image	9
Team Player	9
Life Choices	10
Father Son Talk	11
Chapter 2: An Awful Lot of Scenery	**13**
Bacteria	14
The Gazebo	15
Natural Power	16
Walking in the Rain	16
Snowed In	17
Filling Space	17
Equality	18
Swimmers Ear	18
Clearing the Yard	19
Chapter 3: An Awful Lot of Thee	**21**
You Be There	22
Sun Spots	22
Fishing	23
Dreamer	24
For Melissa	25
Blush	25
Grad	26
Shy Away	27
Trans my Gender	28
Flatus	29
Glory Hound	30
Talk to the Hand	30
Flirt	31
Step Of Love	32
Tough Job	33
My Girlfriend Likes Neruda	33
Fairy Tale Love	34
Indian Bean	35
Call Me Love	36
Foolhardy	36
Angels Named Rachel	37
Jonathan's Verse	38
Young Miss Crabtree	39
Spotty Vox	39
O Fairy Princess	40
Get Together at the Park	40
Sound Bite	41
Chapter 4: An Awful Lot of Need	**43**
Billboard Healthcare	44
Time Out	45
Underpass	46
Humor	46
Rush to What	47
Graffiti	48
Food for Thought	49
Adopt a Pet	49
God Bless the AMA	50
Dear Lad	51
Hang in there Jesus	52
Morning Observations	53

Chapter 5: An Awful Lot of Greed 55

Adam's Apple	56
Greed is Good	57
Plea to the Great Patron	57
Wealth	58
Love Thy Banker	58
The Banker of Kabul	59
Friend Request	59
Onion Board	60
Good Bullet	60
Giving Thanks for the Truth	61
Just Say No	62-63
Tea with Sara	64-65
Just Chilling	66
Speculating the Asp	66
The Hammer Sickle Pickle	67
Persian Gardens	68-69
I'm a Conservative	70
A Slave to Consume	70
Standing Next to the Bonfire but Still Feeling Cold	71

Chapter 6: An Awful Lot of She 73

Grand Design	74
You Are Fair	74
Sitting Quietly	75
No Room in the Freezer	76
S to the M	77
Waking Moments	77
Long Winter	78
Style Denial	78
Footsteps	79
Let's Get Toasted	79
Honest Frustration	80
M	80
Oops	81
Broken Promise	81

Chapter 7: An Awful Lot of Me 83

Inspiration	84
Nature	84
Belief Myself	85
I	85
So Now You Believe	86
The Lazy Despot	86
Quiet the Riot	87
Logic	87
Too Close to Call	88
Baby Steps	88
Shelter Falling In	89
A Touch	89
One Step at a Time	89
No Team in I	90
Steady Boy	90
Exhausted	90
Gummed Up Synapses	91
Sordid Way	91
Disappointment	92
Play Mother Fucker Play	92
A Box	93

Biography 94-97

speak well

little can mean a lot
write word
right time
can hit the spot
change a life
end constant strife

in the beginning
empty was the space
bang
existence came forth
ever forward
life crawling towards the sun
steps taken
first words spoken
drum beats beaten
thumped out repeated
paintings put up on stone sheltered walls
then with charcoal pen
the poet began
rhyme begat reason
the first books
written by them
the true natures of ancient men
hidden within

calm the freshest descent
speaking lightly and politely on the stand
or shaking the right hand
can be something close
held dear
ushering in someone's true New Year
what we do bangs the drum
what we say sings into the future
lighting it like a lamp
warming the damp
store yourself for the moment
avail another with verbal aid
speak well with kindness
in spades you shall be repaid

good books

An Awful Lot of Tree

boob

forgiveness is begged
for I am the one that hurt you
the one that deserted you
disappearing over dollars
a long drive poverty
losing love over money
truly selfish and crass
pushing off so as not to hear your mother's holler
see her choler
I should have begged to wear your collar
laying with you was truth
spitting out your perfection my greatest indiscretion
holding still passion
when the sex is best
hold on to him or her
the true glory in life
is a hot sticky wet mess
a warm breast
and time with the person
that loves you best

loki

play tricks on us
you hairy boy
your heritage ways
not simple toys
pain has carried you
a long hard way
we are truly glad you
decided to stay
serfs in your house
live very well
for your love and protection
are ever-filling wells

my golden dream
licks my face
while her rapid pace
shakes the place
her demands are small
heart gives all
from summer winter to fall
patience and love she will teach us
it is her panting
within our reaches

luna

huff

ah, there lays my lovely
golden helper
helping so well
half-measures are done
but yet somehow whatever the chore
all turns to great fun

when the sunlight hits your
coat of soft shiny armor
you gleam like the sun
oh, and can you run

over my simple lawn mitts
you throw joyful fits
sitting when I say sit
only hesitating a bit

dear sweet pup
I know the day is done
when you've had enough
when you retire to the front of your fan
bed and cushy pillow top
with three wonderful sounds
a snort, an exhale, a huff

applewho? / *loved by one, at least*

ah, to hear your voice
my kind sweet sister's choice
the only one

I believe begun whole
calm
collected
pretty
witty
fun and smart

at present
I will play a tiny part
anon
books
art
music

Chopin a good beginning
The Smiths
Suzie and the Banshees
The Cure

my ears did warm
to
the prettiest voice
God's choice to remind me
of the one important thing
love
you
without some plan
or demand
reaches out your soft lovely hand

change

we are much the same, I've caused you pain
the icy few years chill, a bitter pill
reluctantly swallowed, gulped down the hollow

dearest Sis, I do miss
life has changed me
scary, strange to not during the day
speak your name

my shame

love without true loss is the cost
of growth
living on the other's side of the moat
heights and castles

humble, I wish that I could die
for I have wrung the tear
that now falls from your eye

talking bout money

I was wrong to bring you back to this place
where we started the race
the unforgiving pace
the scary dark space
between us grows
who knows
our lives so subject to which way the wind gusts
it fucking blows
blow after blow after blow
down it all can go
holding on is what I propose
cross our fingers
and we'll make little crosses with our toes

team player

one-way respect
is what you expect
I detect your mind
like an etch-a-sketch

quickly forgetting past aid
as soon as your moment
of need has been laid
my elephant memory
my sense
does not relent
with my help
I am done

when you need a hand
some kind of plan
ask one you have not before met
that would be your best bet

image

driven to excess
two wheels locked
together with steel
me and my leather
the real deal
wind in my hair
iron like stare
I'm a rebel
in my own way
different patches displayed
sparkle my being
not a slave to your modern ways
my only bondage is polishing chrome
three hours a day

what are you going to do
with your life
that's what you say
if I heard you right
day and night
you were born of me
paterfamilias
you can be like me
with the stocks I gave you
just remember son
behave
you be grand
but don't surpass your old man
that wasn't part of the plan

life choices

father son talk

I didn't ask to be your one
spawn, joy or bum
my place was picked in your race
under slight duress, I must confess
I need not be your ace-in-the-hole
your one-man show
yet here I find myself, your pride, your sentimental side
you are driven, have striven at times thoughtfully given
ridden and saved my ass in the past
of you that was very nice
do not regret, you are held dear
but as for my cheer, it has fled
gone sitting quietly in the corner with my leer
let's just sit, talk and have a beer
belay our insecurities, our wariness, our choler
steer the conversation from devotions and emotions
to the latest silly man-made commotions
sit and remember we are father and son
no one said it always must be fun

An Awful Lot of Scenery

bacteria

what dumb luck we crawled from the muck
as pretty a picture
wonderful as a sunrise or
a story from a good book

take a hard look
study the hard read
you may have mistakenly thought
you owned this nook

creatures of all shapes and sizes
crawl and fill every space
not hot, cold, nor wind do we behold
where life is not supported
or at least tries to take hold

dead may be a sea
but to float in its heavy waters
good for thee

this planet will burp, sneeze
and at times ungraciously fart
proving balance by the way of
unwilled death and destruction
terra firma's resurrection, its fresh start
reborn again and again we will,
being born a bore or a thrill

splendid is all, the sea, the sun,
air blown its winded way,
the beach's rocks, stones and natural catacombs

belong
be alone
we all will someday lie softly down
and be spirited quickly home

the gazebo

green iron and lace
set a rapid pace
vines and twines
cover this place
shelter from the light
being right or wrong
the seed's efforts drive is strong
orchids' place is safe
for sweet brothers and sisters
cover for others
and the fragile among us
are held sound

walking in the rain

water pounding concrete
sipping sliding beneath the feet
washing yesterday's shit from the street
riding cycles reaching ends
incomplete spotted oil
upon spots
of trash
of glass
water running down the alleys
ever recurring
never ends
rain
the surfaces' only friend

natural power

speaking truth to flowers
and other natural powers
causes slight allure
one must steer clear
of types of ivy and rue
the mushroom a must
for the fanciful great adjust
combining to richly fill the trust
roughly some tears
twinges and winces will follow
no need to glower
at each experience
you must wonder
think and plunder
so you may avoid
the next
unenlightened
blunder

snowed in

piously standing aside
watching sideways snows
lead by the nose
noticing the beautiful
blow by blow
quivers the holy
earthly sea
gusts of wind impelled along
flakes with multidimensional toes
waltzing their adagios
dancing in the orbs
cold-feathered twisted skies
following blind eyes
as if you please
cities towns and peoples
so quietly brought to rested knees
nature is our mother
with her white blankets
she can and will
blind you like a lover

filling space

feelings of waste
past lives lived steeped in desire's disgrace
egos skinned down to the bone
gnawed on at length
kind of makes you think
RNA the sacred bin where all begin
take a toke it's no joke
bits of
your crazy ass has been around
since men spoke
breath of hot gas
body hair
flesh hugging the spine
conduits divine the curved line
head to toe we are electro chemical
when we are done
the wind we become
floats like spirits settling in and around
bodies of water and ground
waste you're not
you are just caught
like all the other energies and refugees
in this very odd
fifth dimensional spot

AN AWFUL LOT | 17

equality

brought to the brink
way too close to the long dirty stink
six feet of mix and meat
the dirt will assert
our true natures
layers of mineral clay
and assorted hay
dust, rust, fine silks wrap the carcass
open-toed shoes
the Sunday suits
be you blown in the wind
or laying quietly in the shade
under gaudy blocks of stone
stating the letters that made up a name
some earthy saying or claim
you can be a Rockefeller
Bush or McCain
or maybe one of the rest of us
we all end up the same

swimmers ear

starving for a dream
life lived
in-between the seams
right foot grounded
left foot
toes
dangling down
ever testing
Neptune's depths
oceans provide asylum
sinking
smoking
pushing
to the brink
returning to
tell a roundabout story
with bad English and a wink

WILLIAM SICKWITT

clearing the yard

common metal sticks affixed
plumbing the grass for nuggets of the past
the doggy's behind does remind thee of thy place
amongst the plants and other organic wastes
nature's seemingly inglorious face
we are food for thought and others

put in your dime shout over and again
hey that's mine it's mine

reality's ignoble truth
I belong to you as you to me
like the grass belongs to the tree
the arm to the knee
the humble bumble bee
or the parasitic flea
we are a whole on one
all affixed like sticks
in this space
a universe based
on unbounded fumbling grace

An Awful Lot of Thee

you be there

the losses we sustain

losing love

the insurmountable gain

burdens of the lonely

the left behind

empty days

forgotten manners

under warm covers

in dreams they remain

as we inevitably march

towards a picture in the same frame

I will wake still

in but a moment

burdens lastly finally shared

my greatest wish

my only hope

is that you be there

sun spots

you are a star
heat
rays
in forms of radiant
blush
movement
and change
as the solar surface moves
I move
your effects evident
from your heart
your heat
I must run
because I could so easily spend
the rest of my days
wanting what could never be mine
sitting all day
staring at the sun

fishing

the ill spoken word
to singular many others sounds absurd
not unlike I, thee does not deny
statement from lies both tend to disguise
learning lawyer's truth enables one to stand
subjectively at the smart peoples' booth
answering questions masses have in common
I care not for untruth unless for the eye or from on high
comforting words from stern spiritual guides
tasting as familiar as vanilla pie
a mistruth consists of itself
a character a sleuth with which to act, to play
place it in a small boat and let it float, wash away
on the shore it lands, runs aground
commotions emotions induced
you know you've found
the person state or town where your problems may be found
hooked linked to the chain line
up the inane to blame
and those responsible that you should reckon
and when the time is proper beckons
calculate how in the world to stay sane with shame
in a sordid silly fractional game where everyone is to blame

dreamer

day dream of mine

sweet, blessed and kind

all that could be desired

grace is not enough to describe

soft skin from head to beautiful toe

wisdom, intelligence and natural elegance

with not a hint of ego

touching your body

grazing thy heart

your ways, movements

like art

when you call me Will

my soul goes still

then begins the song

it sings a melody

your name repeated

if only you could belong

be my prize

O lovely light in my eyes

for melissa

as platinum is your blond
your beauty as gracious
strong as your bond
in class both in time
you will journey will fly
your dreams will start like the sun

blush

I see in your eyes
we have met before
sweet lovely girl
did you see my heart jump
the planets warned me of your effects
settling with a tour
ins and outs
exquisite limbs and lips
crimson-balanced cheeks
blushing left to right
one next to one
makes two

grad

cap and gown worn this day

reached through hard works

mountains of books

and mind numbing essays

difficult times and constant measures

dotted with flights of selfish pleasures

travel amongst the rabbles

constant worries and joys wrapped in a handsome

brown-headed boy

ascertain the official channels of learned babble

and when sitting in chairs of power

in starlit ivory towers

remember your humble beginnings

and for the sake of the tip

don't forget the happy endings

shy away

no need to shy away
I do desire you under
me
my touch my grasp my sway
yet with your emotions I do not wish to play

yes my glance is for you
secrets are not safes and
do not always hold
yes your hand I wish to hold
reaching out to you risky and bold

the slender little black dress fits you well
as for me you've no need to sell
I want you
to hold
to taste
to smell

others always demand from you
to drive
to shop
to sit on the side of their lines
that's no dream of mine

my only want is to see you at ease
no little black dress
wet from a shower
white t and juicy sweats
parts of your body resting on my chest
that would be best

trans my gender

Aphrodite loves you best
she chose to feather your nest
with much more than the rest
the goddess of love and war measured your gifts
with some great inner and outer conflicts
in loving one's self, all is absolved
trans is my gender, mi amour, my splendor
I love things from the blender
tasting salty and sort of sweet
like the beautiful different people we meet
quality is your light, you are special, you are right
those who appall are just tiny and small
in centuries on this planet
they have grown an inch or not at all
you being little of one, some of the other
fits you like a wonderful cover or
a sensitive savvy two-handed lover
you were born with balance and talents
both worlds mixed together, what could be better
lovely you are there standing
long shaven legs sexy aft
heels, short skirt and a tight sweater
acceptance for all is coming quite late
as for me I think you all are great

flatus

breaking wind
where should I begin
of the all perfectly natural acts
of this people quickly react
fuming over common indiscretions
gas-filled noxious earthly emissions
filling the sheets couches and meetings in our lives
with smirks giggles and at times great pride
walking down the bookstore aisle you unknowingly fall
into someone's remnant natural bluster
still full of power and luster
you inhale choke and gasp
then move with all the celerity you can muster
they can slither silently like the Egyptian asp
sneaking upon you like your past
why people get so upset I don't know
it's just a little wind that had settled in your belly
and just happened to come out your back end
sweetly scented oxygen

glory hound

my desire for glory the oldest story
moth to the flame
some kind of footprint
wishing to mate color and frame
at least I'll leave a dirty name
being sick with witt my sordid claim
offending you to think
shocking you to blink
I love the pink
shades of red in your cheek
I wish to make you warm
a form of hot steam
blown up your skirt
to hurt is human it keeps you alert
looking how you do
why shouldn't I flirt

talk to the hand

as you drove your hand into the sky
I felt the wisp of self-serving air pass by
understanding you speak
I understand it is so you may later run and cry
to those whom sit on high
to protect your patchy reputation
you spit in my eye
I shall not give of my temper my time
with grizzle yammer or whine
I'll bide my time
place you snugly in the pages and ages
of a mean-spirited yet fitting rhyme
where you will rest
for all time
looking as you naturally do

knowingly deaf
instinctively dumb
and purposefully blind

inappropriate is my glare
being aware of your person
measured feet away
hair gently falling behind your ear
eyes bright searching calm
mannered ways displayed
lovely long neck
Starbucks collar resting on your breast
middle covered in black
tan corduroy pants, the luckiest pair
holding your wonderful seat in its warm pockets
belt brown and thick, the buckle the second lock I wish to pick
gladly I wait for a drink, time to write, to think, to dream
all my intellection was of you standing in view
as discreetly as a wanton man could
I took from you a picture
subtle curves, ivory skin, sweet welcoming arms
reaching a beautiful end
as a strange man monopolized your time
I wish your eyes
your neck
your lips
bottom and thighs
and all you comprise

step of love

step with me from this ledge
tis to fall by your side
my pledge
together let's repose
touch gently our toes
edging forward
to balance
scraping ahead
sand stone and air
fall
trickling down
the gorges hall
coming to rest upon the river
and its long-sunken bed
down
centered in the canyon's crack
just above the water's bottom
take a deep breath sexy girl
let's get right
get stoned
sweet love and leap
assured if we hold on to each other
we will land on our feet

tough job

vivid is my recollection
passing with flying colors
playfulness and passion
beautiful frames
always in fashion

vestal ladies
greeting each other
the afterlife
if something like this room
will be rocking nice

adorning the walls
clear plastic busts
park north
celebrations of where
the breasts rest
under which I see your lovely heart
is beating
brightening
this well-lit room
forty-two plus

my girlfriend likes neruda

bearded child
still haven't found your way
this late in the day
clerk at the counter
counter at the clerk
I'm buying the Captain's verses
no need to be a jerk
I just want to buy this half-priced book
not to look up your skirt
to make eye contact is not to flirt
you infantile
small minded twerp

fairy tale love

how, dear lad, could you love a sheep?
laying with wool
makes for itchy sleep
carnal love and sex
the cost so steep
if intent you are on such a dastardly, bestial deed
least you could do
is name her
Little Bow Peep

indian bean

raised in the shade
riding both sides
of the human parade

two-sided mask worn
inches above your lazy ass
loyalty your undeserved word
great communist you would be
Stalin your work
should have stayed the age of three
diapers and feedings
scheduled for thee

you cry foul as others
take pride in their balanced side
your belly aches and hurts
at the thought of work

ushering fourth the one-sided alerts
for trusting you I deserve scorn
for I had been warned
jealousy is the felony
with which you have been cursed
it's not my way
if one is to fuck another over
It's you that shall be first

call me love

before I knew your name
you called me love
ruby lips
raven hair
olive skin
beautiful
brave enough
to unflinchingly gaze upon my eyes
your lovely heart open
pressing against my chest
midline, I stand in line
offering only
desperate prose
strong hands
near poverty
and worn out clothes
that don't care to match
a body
you may press too
grand dreams
lots of green
Angels need not spread their wings
to heal a broken man it seems they
need only say one thing

                                  laying supine
                             in this wilderness
                                a song brings
                                        memory
                                    your voice
                                  side by side
                                  next to me
                        compassion empathy
                                         foolish
                            dreamers like me
                                      can be
                            to give my life
                                        to you
                 as simple as you please
                            my only alibi
                              it's happened
                                    already
                                     before

                               in my dreams

foolhardy

angels named rachel

I was delivered a wounded seraph
falling for nine months, she landed here in my modern lap
never had I questioned my back how strong it could be
what weight it could bear
fear of death comes for all
but ever constant worry of the leaves dropping so early in the fall
storm clouds moving, swirling, forcing rains showers of tears
quickly aging one and all the erudition, the involution of fear
charged with the care of a Fabergé child
a fragile porcelain gift the splendid burden
from this, steps forward there is not return
women like we carry mankind
children of men men who are children
unique little girls with tight little curls
them bearing the weights and measures of worlds
little Rachel's spine is much stronger than mine
when she performs her songs it is divine
the young boys the loving kin
are men for being near her for days on end
I sit and gaze upon you my beautiful egg
marveling at how wonderful you are
and how it is in life when things can go so terribly wrong
how they can be so right
and such a marvelous wondrous sight

jonathan's verse

too quickly I slipped from your grasp
too soon
too fast
too quietly cast

in the middle of
high school nights
hearing of dancing near
sharing our smiles made of light

beautiful future joined
held in common
like strong white teeth
or lovely brown hair

Jimmy and the Doors
Bill's stacks of records

together always to amuse
with just a
once and awhile
good natured brotherly
verbal goose

my grin is for you
mother and father times two
parents had part
hard on the heart
but I always had you

hear I
standing nearby smiling
amazed at your ever growing beauty
always about around
like a loving memory

in forms of spirit
like when the sun ends
as when it begins
my presence shall be felt by you
yet again

as you sit surrounded by
beaches sun and good friends
scents of the ocean

by giggling auburn crowned
children

I am latter-day
and my love for you
may change its forms
it's manners

but it never ends

spotty vox

I hear the lilt
the tilt
in your spoken word
changing your voice
displays your choice
the lyre played beside the fire
singing the uneven song
dancing in between the wood
the unbalanced flame
you may think we are the same
the thought inane
I'm certainly crazy
but luckily not
viscous fictitious or clinically insane

young miss crabtree

the bitch with an itch
a bad memory
embarrassment shame and misery

the unknown a scary thing
especially while feeding on your
one and only irreplaceable thing

the largest member of my club
it feels great to rub even in the tub
when it's in distress I cannot rest

cooling creams laundry a plenty
smelly medicine hair
combing ones self with Barbie's tiny brush

no sir no sir
yet again I will not rush
to the house of the girl I itch to touch

o fairy princess

O fairy princess
I feel your winces
you care not
for goblin kind
those not of holy design
they fit ill in that tiny space
the sheltered place
of dress of grace
a few barons and many squires
visit you all twelve nights
dazzle you saddle you rattle you
many colors weave thy tapestry
then you left behind
tis not a tragedy
that special wish
it will come true
Prince Charming
you will find
he'll be emotionally unstable
and if he's lucky blind

the only thing we have to fear
is each other
mans so-called brother
will nail you to a cross for a lover
a simplistic business measure
or for sadistic pleasure
yeah
I'll go reunions to treasure
then again
I think I'll hang at home
smoke a bowl or two
or three
read write
and with the past
agree to disagree

get together at the park

WILLIAM SICKWITT

sound bite

Beautiful buxom blondes
foxes on stage looking like
Eva Brauns
lying upright strait-faced
unlaced

The man from down under
bent on imposing
 his special kind of reeve
freedom for his well-dressed class
not your common skinny ass

Standing atop empire
sycophants aplenty
owning the house out back
and many now too low cost
blue aerial waves

Servile most should be
freedom to think
wounds double-sided monopoly
what's bad for the deal
no good for you
no good for me

The most comfortable beds
are feathered with insider threads
soundly sleeping upon mounds
of tangible riches
knowingly growingly cozen

Be wary be careful my dear tan friend
of the seeds one sows
they grow in chartless directions
and like all Frankenstein monsters
ogres often kill and devour
those who are close
those who they know

An Awful Lot of Need

billboard healthcare

little Brooke loves her new pacemaker,
billboard Sony big-screen
and special-occasion dressmaker
little Shaniqua got a new heart in a different way,
she got to meet her maker,

mac and cheese, inner cities and heart failure.
advertising coins and catheters cost lives.
what would society be without competition
unequal sides
home owners associations
white
and all other kinds of pride?

care be not universal
like market shares
Kathy survived her cancer,
she had money
that's the answer
how many bandages does a billboard buy?
marketing execs get paid bonuses
while people needlessly die
the American way
the American lie

time out

It's a lovely corner you put me in
rhyme for the time out, let's begin
you are so special, so true
you are holier than when, but certainly not now
you are grown, have won
and two plus two
noble ears and eyes shoulders arms
many charms
hormones a measurable difference
but we shan't be flippant
with some things we must not joke
the inside outside corner of this school, church or home
greeted upon me is pretty and nice
but terribly short of actual spice
flavor is the true labor
worth living working for

making fun with shame is a
dangerous foolish game
turn round the corner
back from anger
back from force
a place should be greater than a recess
a human stall
funnel-shaped numbskull caps at times worn by all
forgive yourself and others
we mess up, we falter
understand dear teacher, parent or preacher
righteousness is a tried and true slow-witted plan
staring at the walls that I command
what I see, where I stand
everyone that walks under the light
has the right to be
whomever the hell they like

underpass

as drivers quickly pass above
held up by molded stone pillars
shield the carcasses of the dead
and the almost living
Target carts filled
with meaningless objects
loosely called to belong
sit together with
the odor of pigeon shit
it's sticky and strong
shaded by freeways
walking along
the shores of river of Styx
for those who won't belong

humor

with warm tepid breath
I spoke the words
unsympathetic and weak
as the poor woman sat
shaking in worries
addiction misery and defeat
the overwhelming self
classic tongue and cheek

rush to what?

to sheltered sun
the day begun
many run
pacing drafting and racing
rubber metal aluminum
hurry I say
do not delay
captive foolish fortunes
could wash away
with safety and security
you must not play
others we bump
shove and pinch their behinds
threaten everyone's lives on our morning
and afternoon drives
what do we really save
in the scheme of daily things
but a little bit
of meaningless time

graffiti

I was here

spit from a can, staining the walk,
a little bit in the middle,
some ends reaching out to the side

I walked over your plea without great care,
yet a thought, like spray paint remains,
lingers like drugs in hair

slipshod is your painting on the crude cement way,
but be glad with your art,
you wish to partake, to create

city elders and sidewalks should not be
so surprised when marks and displays
cover their paseos

turn-table tapestries are signs from God,
purple spotted esplanades convey
I have something to say

for art and the future of the species
we must pay whatever the cost.
without models of beauty in all its forms
and shapes, the future is gray and lost

food for thought

frosty comfort
ripping flesh from the bone
granite statues of flawed men
feel of home
dominating cousins
one or a dozen
matters not
doctrine and policy
must play their part
in the plot
for to be or not
it's a sobering thought
please just lay there
maybe on the little gray cot
Soylent Green a silly B drama
yet to the facts I do react
should I be so bold
if it's perfectly acceptable for us
to eat our young
why not the old?

adopt a pet

nobility walks about with six legs

messy t-shirts
extra long hot days

the one constant
we all wish but
love
respect
a hug
a hand to the cheek
the occasional treat

let's share
the open spaces
in our minds and hearts
get to know
a soul

take a walk together
you may find
a friend
a love
that you don't wish to let go

god bless the ama

the Hippocratic oath, an old lawyer-like joke
Hippocrates an aged old fool who didn't know of modern schools
how expensive pedagogy would be
and of what riches and status you could achieve
when not just trading others' health for salt beads and goats
but luxury cars, homes and boats
the association and its members give tit
to those who will later give tat
protecting their futures
and those of their educated grade
doing just enough good
so common folk will sit on their seats quietly in the lobby
and to the wanton obstructions
not make hay
doctors doing their best with cash and coat hanger in hand
to abort any universal health care gain, advance or plan
tis their special right
they touch with God's hands
the wellbeing of our nation can be looked past
what's truly important is their sophisticate class
caring about your fiscal wellness is not part of your insurance plan
for not making enough money
or living cleaner lives
those families sick and in need should rightfully go by the wayside

dear lad

O carry on dear lad
it takes such great effort to be so heavy hearted, so sad
shallow depth hold you surround
you the still troubled waters hue of purple green
envelop like no other
chafing inwardly and out
at the great rat race, your caste
the line in which you were placed
the queue where all must wait
fair is only a version of skin
it is a simple lie, like sin
others preach, beseech
give us your hand, we shall commit thee to the lamb
you are their fodder
their constant contest
their noble slaughter
your self and wealth is the wish
filling the Sunday meetings and silver plate
only you can hold yourself high
you are the one, the sun
deny your fears, accept humanity
some tears stand without aid
open to love
in spades, ye shall be repaid

hang in there jesus

stapled to some form of maple
hung like the sun
sand scrub rock dust and stone
lay beneath your feet

hanging around without holding on
quite a feat
what a terrible way to end a day
this is the thanks you get
for asking people to do what you say

death does not always mean a licking
followers of your way still count your days
laity get stiff at the knees and pray
try to be human and still live your day

mumble their tongues
exclaim your name from their lungs
dusty smelling Sunday Sabbaths
wholesome family fun

for the hard-working clergy
hefty retirement funds
whole lives built and lived
off your one day in the sun

spirit just begun

morning observations

turkey bacon if I am not mistaken
sitting
standing the morning down
the digest express
a few short stacks of years

sitting over easy
writing not so

wanabe gangste
texting a yard from me
hops on a waitress
for a miniscule slip
berating someone working hard
that doesn't even make eight

reality's great miss
forgiveness
a funny thing
half-Asian gangster
texting your master
looking like a hairless ape

she'll put up with your
whiny ass
it's just part of her day
if you look at her name tag
it says Faith

An Awful Lot of Greed

adam's apple

my belief is in numbers
only every fifteen years or so they blunder
if the bottom falls out, it's ok
the ass that hauls the load
stands with little clout
it carries the same burden
whether wood, water or some oversized lout

indexing a voluntary treason
no one free rides for Freidman
when the best way to safeguard our freedom
paper driven mechanical equilibriums
suckling infant industries
some two-hundred years young
corporate trusts can go on and on and on

we must nurture treasure and
protect the fragile ones
we can be dismal and great
like a sound exchange rate
tottering here at the low end of the Phillip's curve
it's my uneducated choice
it's what I deserve

for me, no pork for free, no tariffs or barriers
protecting my house my car, my special areas
dear Adam Smith, you've given us
this great patented gift
if only I had been lucky enough
to be born a financial wizard, spendthrift
or humble economist

plea to the great patron

greed is good

O cherished Harvard square
I couldn't help but stare
lovely ivy-covered towers
finely manicured lawns
poetry-loving girls named Fawn
it is your special place
choosing who is left who is right
spent days on the islands
cabins and lakes of the master race teaching others their
rightful caste
rowing five minutes quicker
dark robes stretching fabric
east to west
sacred blood staining
tattooing family crests
my plea to shine with you
oh gated ones
and those who share your
grand mutual funds
I promise to protect your claims
fight kill or die to protect your
capital gains

a tall man stood leaning
against a palisade of plenty
was begged for a twenty
his tie turned white
off went the light
deftly he spoke
"those in need are not so bright
for men of affairs avarice is need
my beloved street's founding creed
the dismal science I am reliant
to your ragged bitter end
this wall like my investors win or lose
does not bend
if you wish to spend
earn it or steal it, like I do
my poor, wholly wretched friend"

AN AWFUL LOT | 57

wealth

grand designs are pretty and fine
shame they are yours
not ours or mine
even pennies well spent do not make mortgages or rent
landlords' riches the trick
humming along making business tick
percentages must grow for those in the know
lasting knowledge must go
progressive is the past
old ways will not last
drowned by the markets
in little wooden foreign-made baths
once they've gotten their piece of the ass
on they move, it's called class
let's make the deal
it's a bargain, a steal
owning the earth
its riches will get you the bitches
prop up your futures with wills that can last
man-made inflations raising your stations
raising the rents beloved fifteen percents
buying lands money well spent
better than throwing cash in holes
like the lowly people paying the rents

> men in machines
> many zeros
> plenty ones
> the blessed gift
> of atomic fun
> America is beautiful
> it is free
> at least as far
> as eyes can see

love thy banker

the banker of Kabul

with a buttons push
goes your Kush
our shared ghosts
tucked away in Khost
many hidden paper warnings
margins lost in hoarding
small print is great
if you own the heaviest paper weight
America's bearded turban covered tool
sheltered
doomed away
so we can safely play the fool
pretty flowers fill in the long dark hours
fueling growths on the winding silk markets
what must the patriotic mercenary lad do
nothing dear Kidd
he is our friend our mate the banker of Kabul

friend request

step lightly onto the future
it's a mega computer
constructing stacking numbers
trolling our data
booking times and places with faces
family friends and races
it comes in stages
before you know it
you and yours
are locked in cages

onion board

the lot of you
laying there rotting
plotting your next step
the wind has not blown long
quick enough to dry your eyes
some not so sad
while living and breathing
you brought tears, made many cry
being reliant, you turn out for millions
this your reward--put out on holey ironing board
decay not all we mention
not so unpleasant as an unworthy thought
sweet onions and shallots
we love you and hold you
chastise you and scold you cut you up
as for mother and I
we are glad you are here
to add flavor to our lives
and ripen our pots

good bullet

it's not a worthy bullet unless you pull it
snap thud measured clank
spinning with scientific ease
such is the monopoly on fetching true velocity
the breathtaking capture holy rapture
the richest case hidden in a six-digit place
a calculated lick aim and click
not such a simple trick
before we meet that being their last thought
one thousand steps
must be sought researched and bought
noble-sized profits at cost is the mission
controlling populations and sheeples the vision
noble if only on paper
powder and keg for king country and caste
spending a round brass ringing as it hits the ground
O what a gilded sharp sound
give this tailored ushered world time
I soon shall be divine

WILLIAM SICKWITT

little old man
spending all your time with the truth
fidgeting with frail souls and
your retirement goals
> Religionist's phone banks
> many thanks
> finding satisfaction in steeples
> and misguided peoples

Christ from a can
spilled out onto your hands
verbal beliefs you bequeath
to like-minded muggins
all heads buried in ancient sands
> tis with the white burkas you will not worship
> evil cousins shall not be thrown
> the blessed rope
> white girls loving turbans
> not worthy of your words
> your second-hand hopes

some Disciples of Christ
must spend minutes
hear the rites
so they may know light from night
a deservedly bovid plight
> like mine on this holiday night
> at thanksgiving dinner I sit
> and at the head of the table
> a well-thought-of
> grey-templed nit-wit

giving thanks for the truth

just say no

God loves you boys and girls
Little Billy, Suzie, Joey
Kimberly and Stan
you are our labor
our love
fed with mothers breasts
the food earned fathers hands

'tis due to your self-indulgent nature
we must now restrain and detain you
hold you like chattel with the help of
your heavily armed Uncle Sam
your faults have ruined fond memories
of The Brady's, the Cosby's
and easy imaginary American family plans

thankfully heaven has graced us with
Nancy Reagan's saintly being
she and her friends must know life's true meaning
they are moral and the majority
phony phone banks galore
so go forth do as you're told, crusade
subjugate your small fry's
America's children
their cousins their friends
 your neighbors your kin

the violent state that's never been close to won
together sung with the sound of black boots
stomping to the door
we can finally win

letting people breath honest
be themselves to err
WJWD
an unprofitable unforgivable sin

victory is so close if you just cage
your clan in orange and grey
bottled up with true violence, illness and hate
metal hugs not drugs
prison backrubs
two cheap meals three cigarettes a day

generous prison lobbies and owners get paid
and off the backs of our non-violent slaves
money like plane reservations can be made
costs can be saved bonuses can be paid

choirs in our country constantly sing
hand over heart we are number one
USA USA USA
but yet there you stand with
shiny badge, black boots, black helmet
scope and deadly weapon
pointed at your future
your daughters your sons

those who profit keep unhealthy
politicians, laws afloat
playing on the fears of those aging
who actually vote

brothers kill your brother
friend turn on your friend
sign this piece of paper
betray your world
or we will be your end

the war on drugs
the war without end
a million more times
hateful, destructive and harmful
then some fucked up selfish addiction

tea with sara

I call on you, Honored Chancellor Laurel
and good Minister Hardy,
if you love your country, sign this card
pay a miniscule fee and unite with the tea bag party

Change we can't believe in, is the reason,
stand side-by-side we will,
as in the golden age of that Boston spill
Revolutionaries we will be,
if you dip your tender bag next to me
in the historically hot waters of history.

Feathered quills and beautiful parchment too high
a cost, so tis alongside our brethren we slowly walk
to rail against governments over-reaching power
with cardboard posters and marks-a-lot

Thwarted we have been by our friends at homeland
security, not free to hide in barrels, paint our faces,
no Indian feathers on our dress
decidedly no fun but on the flip-side
the least amount of effort is best,
in case our brethren spill their
Bud Lights, Millers or Schlitz.

Don't worry about the message lost,
Fox news will fill the shot
so massive crowds fill the back lot,
and even the badly-spelled
held upside-down message,
will get its wide shots.
herding misguided sheeples
conveniently filling empty manmade time slots.

Tea baggers believe in all we were taught,
that America should rule the world at any cost,
we have the right to work so hard
we tie our stomachs in knots,
for satellite TV and the privilege to shop at Big Lots.

Some of the English way crowns our plight,
the reason for our independent frown
may be the idea that
the country is lead by someone
not like our crowd, but a little brown.

So it's up from the couch
from the political slouch
whether we cared was in doubt,
now we're out, hoping the streets
will support our stout.

We stand for freedom when the day provides sun,
it's with t-shirts and flip-flops all insurrections are
won, to understand a thing we have just begun;
reading a book? We've heard it's fun.

We have the right to march in sight
and not to shelter our sound,
even if our ideas are upside-down;
like herpes we've spread the message
to many cities and towns.

We who stand and watch the march
go by, get the point, the USA
was better two hundred years ago
when you could lock people in cages
and taxes were decidedly low.
sorry, tea baggers, we and our
progressive friends aren't going to go.
intelligent ones are now guiding the show.

just chilling

how do you like the
third world
rolling blackouts
haven't you heard
deregulation
what a cool
money making word
the rich get richer
as we suffer the blizzards and snow
burr
Texas politicians sold us out
energy lobbies have actual clout
the priority is cash
not keeping the cold out

speculating the asp

curious creature millions of scales
touching all mandibles
unfastened one-way lawless
swallowing nest eggs whole
forked tongues
tickling the luckless greedy
the reptiles wants and needs
bounty for a margin fee
partial system whispered inner warnings
venom nestled between the lines
deadly poisons process hard to digest
numbing the body and brain
thinning the investor's counts
the middle-man's gain
us or them they feel no shame
it is the viper and snake
that tout their parasitic fair shake
valid excuse for rape
feeling vibrations the fall is felt
the occasional catastrophic break
selling short in the trees they go
avoiding the major blow
how wonderful it is
to be cold-blooded
and in the know

the hammer sickle pickle

the chill down my spine is not by design
thinking of bone-cold days
stinking, reeking of gloriously tended Eastern ways
the dry polar skin frozen to the touch
cutting down the pathways strait to the thalamus
causing chained white slaves to protect their ways
going with the status quo trained by our dear loving Uncle Joe
Tsar Stalin a master baiter, would toss his line, feel a tug then nudge,
then wrap you in a rug--feeling, holding, gripping your lasting place
so many keen works of sadness, depression and madness
slowly infusing, infecting the human race
as unseen great stocks, whole peoples blindly jumping through countless Potemkin steeples
keeping centuries of want and waste
it's the picturesque beauty of a socialist soviet state
always bearing in mind, loving your brother
like fucking your mother, sure at first it's great
but Mendel's lines would bargain--the bubble will burst
and you'll be first to have your devious head on a plate
as Yezhof will tell you, your neighbor will sell you
so they may evade their fair share of the stake
so sell no meat no cheese no eggs
a mindset fashioned for dregs
O great hairy bear living on unbounded wilderness
why did sweet Psyche provide you your station on a frozen foundation
bleed your fine people of the rights of man
or the simple satisfaction of a lasting tan
we feel for you dear selfish mother Russia
your great empire gone the moment your wayward son Lenin signed on

persian gardens

grandfather, you would look marvelous walking in green.
the gardens planted by your ancestors,
tended by you, flourish in the light;
greeted by new days, ways, and means.
soil and sand of many kinds,
mixed together, fed with knowledge,
watered with tears, held in and
poured from soft loving hands.
it is of you honored ones we must
make small honest heartfelt demands.

we of your family tribe and tradition,
we who carry your blood
walk in the city's pathways composed,
hoping for small freedoms repose.
you need not beware your green young,
moving through dark streets
painting every door hang,
speaking to wisdom beyond their years,
with infinite compassion
and the noblest love.

great fathers we stood with you as bombs fell
on Abadan, Tehran and Khoramshahr.
husbands , men of the of the nation fought
as Persian mother's danced, arms raised in the air,
singing songs of joy and happiness
so our offspring, our joined future not be afraid,
yes, we too remember those days,
heads bowed in prayer, voices raised in praise.

we have come to this,
bloody hands of men kneeling
as dark-haired voices lay
on this lovely garden soil bleeding,
as brown eyes call out for forgiveness
and justice to the divine.
all while green-stemmed roses and tulips
in every Persian city mature and bloom,
walking arm in arm like
intertwined vines in solid lines.

as ever-patient Damavand peers down,
guests not, but strangers hide
in the open doors of other's homes,
breathlessly quiet,
brothers giving their clothes
as cover from night's authoritarian,
unforgiving predictable freeze.
it is only God, that has the right
to bring a people to their knees.

fathers please knock down some earthen walls,
design more passages,
walkways in this beautiful garden,
and make room for all.
join us in these sacred steps dearest elders;
it is our great Islamic republic,
independence and freedom
in the end that you forestall.

i'm a conservative

dangerous is the eighty IQ
those who can put together two plus two numbering three
the whole picture never in view
dissections haphazardly made
hurt me
hinder you
the peaceable state being hard for many to relate
forcing the unforgivable course
bred into generations of warhorses
uniformed bridals and bits
stagnantly our nation sits
status quo
the love of dough
the first Cesar yell's from the grave
the nation state must maintain behave
empire can last if you learn from the past
steal the best from the rest
conquering with humane laws
burning more bras
secular calls
the best education for all
learn to crawl
to walk to run to fly
Americas only chance to survive

a slave to consume

we but slaves to consume
the inevitable doom
you
me
free
if only to be
it's not so bad
as I can see
tastes vary
the dirty bits are scary
there's no need for excessive worry
solace will be found
in the profound
hands held
and someday in the cool ground

WILLIAM SICKWITT

black helicopters
in circled flight
towering walls of sound
cattle cars parked on hallowed ground
spent rounds abound
delusions of grandeur and common pedophilia
do long haired prophets wear
lies on behalf of misguided civil servants
put U.S. tanks on American ground
the stage set for the burial mound
pride and entitlement the fall of all
Christ Koresh could have been arrested strolling through town
sending an age old message our employs burned them down
carved stone crosses of all sizes now lay
under which twenty one lambs of God
and fifty-four Christian zealots can be found
as ghosts of our freedoms dance effortlessly around

standing next to a bonfire but still feeling cold

An Awful Lot of She

grand design

you heal without regard

love grown like nature

blooming in the sun

warm dry shelter from the rain

walking together

your hand given mine

held without limits

grows like the wiry passion vine

legs up wallowing in the all important rut
like a midsummer night's dream
clean driven like a stream
blue jeans a blouse of many greens
how could you fathom what you mean
twelve legs up
ten hairy don't be wary
I stare for you are a sight
my loving part Cherokee wife
without you there would be a lesser me
less times three
care dare aware
sweet beautiful girl
you are fair
my loving muse
should you choose to keep me
you may abuse
like shoes wear me out
without doubt
my oath I am your oaf
thanking everything that
of all of your faults
I am one

you are fair

WILLIAM SICKWITT

sitting quietly

I see your eye

glancing down

I see your thigh

nestled just steps from you

I see your fingers long and slender

I see them touching lightly grasping

the New York Times weekender

you are my splendor my blender

mixing minds and frames with you

has made me great

turned me in

I see your graceful moves the way you pick

the way you choose

I'm with you win or lose

I don't yet see all of you

from my wayward obstructed view

no room in the freezer

God damn it wife you've filled my life
with love, work and intermittent strife
filling the spaces and places
with belongings and longings
the cold box filled to the brim
so we shall not be skinny, starving or grim
I am so many times ranting and raving
considering your spending and savings
intelligent ways always thinking of future days
I stand shoving, pressing, pushing against
your mind, your love then pausing with regret
seeing the light that you are more
than many nights right
the words I say do not convey
a heart and freezer full of hard earned bounty
on which we now belay
God damn it wife, fixed to you I am
bound of love and life
till the frost-bitten end

moments to the m

frankly I wish you to spank
me
for a little fee
cut me down
as one would
a rotted tree
bending at the knee
so you may deliver
blows
one two three
counting patently
til blisters almost be
feathered touch to light
does not feel like home
perhaps another night
this the hour
to train me
restrain me
hold me tight
abuse helps me feel right
tis a memory
shaped like a scar
like
principles offices
or
lighting bugs
trapped in a jar

waking moments

while in my sleep choirs sing dream-like songs of you
white black grey and gold blanket the room
down pillows act as reigns of our polished sleigh
the dark wood nightly holding safe may be one
maybe two three or four
tis in moments in waking glimpsing through gently lit darkness
I notice you
chest and breasts rise and fall covered by piles of white comfort rolled atop my queen
as she slumbers she lifts she dreams
my lover then squeaks shuffles and rustles
to the beat of 400 counts softly played
whatever held the day
at night next to you
is where I wish to lay

long winter

spring is not to come
trust is spent

what was once done undone
for boundaries admittedly I am not one

I sit in the rain and stare at the sun
unhappiness and day dreams
make for some fucking strange mood swings
long days and easily broken gold rings

style denial

bits of scrap paper stained with blood
and ink blotches from the next and last
holding our days still
many memories held fast
present throwing itself into
an unseen tomorrow
yet unrecorded past
tell the time of a rhyme like
staking a claim on
an old salt mine
the sweet rein
my dear loving wife
thee being foolish
sensible masochistic and kind
rehearsing my verses I sit
inwardly laughing
giggling at your ways
your wit
and how perturbed you get
when I utter my verbal butter

footsteps

We four walked
quietly in the breeze
twelve legs strolling
our skin surfaces covered
by coats of pain, hurt and loss
six years or so
done
tossed
what love you had for me
in your bosom
is empty
hollow
and we
as the old oak tree
eaten up by hours
fighting for silly non-existent
powers
none of which means
anything
anymore
especially
at this late hour

the one who once
loved thee
now runs from me
hides like the owl
past fortune telling her future
ringing useless bells
living through leveled hells
yet I but wish her well
everyone falls
has fell
here's
a bowl
a drink
a toast
to the end of a long
dry spell

let's get toasted

honest frustration

I hear you right
the sky is bright light
in the middle of the night
the flat gray rock is a bird
the moon is made of butter curd

the rules are made and followed
by the honest deaf and shallow
always sensitive to races
special needs cases

stiff are the voice and face
eyes elsewhere misplaced
scanning for an exit
in case the lie degenerates

the wood we walk on is bone
ones work should be a home
the air is laughing gas
everyone has a special ass

I love you
I'm with you
truth be told at times it gets old
I regretfully fumble and mumble
the ugly fact well known
we often find ourselves
standing alone
with no Windex or paper towels
in a glass house as a home

my best moments belong to you
your face smiling is what I have seen
when I was granted glimpses of my nobility
joined national holidays covered by love
miles of walks
intelligent talks
tired puppies
sore feet
I the first to truly
turn your head
yes it is possible
someone had you read
I miss you
breathing in my bed
I wish you to know
although deeply hurt
my love will never leave you
it will only end
when I'm dead

oops

ah the Freudian slip
turning right
the drip drip drip
I loved you once
more than any
finished quickly
leaps bound up in gravity
both feeling weighted down
solace mired in sorrow
each looking out for their own tomorrow
I hadn't dawned shiny armor
 learned where to mark
the dots dashes and commas
to prevent head traumas
I don't want the Bahamas
 just shade
warm bodies
 and a corner
 with no drama

fill my empty ears with spite
if you feel you have the right
under this light
I will grow
water your grounds with money
faux fear and disquieted silence
with simple things
your love and care you invest
in
objects
I will work to create
of beauty
from the forge of your anger
fired
added by the oldest of friends
loneliness and desire
don't fret
you will quickly find
another lonely
hapless buyer

broken promise

An Awful Lot of Me

inspiration

within my depression
seated with joy anger and repression
lays disturbed
ham-fisted inspiration
blindly stumbling towards
nothing
but phrases formed together
molded into cheap plan praises
explicit verses softly coerce
steam like pressures
building as stones
stacked upon each other
held up by tawdry
weak-willed garden gnomes
envisioning the burst
dirty bits of flying verse
exposing day dreams and fault
all inching towards the long haul
the long stay
I get it now
that's why people dream
that's why they pray

nature

the origins and natures of my disasters
set firmly in the skills I have not mastered
many ill-fitting goals floating dropped
into unregulated, unlearned shoals
stepping stones lightly feel
little slip
stuck in muddy habits past
cravings, addictions held fast
inches of learning pulled forward by rub
death the measured step disavowed
not allowed
cheating fleeting urges repeating
forced to continue breathing
self
lying, cheating, deceiving
shines the tunnel bright
turning out the good book
allegories
purposefully not right
they serve others out of sight
invisible chains fastened tight
have no fear
it is safe in here
where there is no light and truth held dear
it's just another night

belief myself

fixated on the unrelated
focused on but hocus-pocus
daydreams of despotic naked utopias
as the keep costs grow more steep
one fails to get relief

frightful numbered steps
tip-toe around the inept
as waves of days
gently consume
turning you up and down in and out
making you doubt

draw back your fears
wet future assured
the drought will not hold out
breakers look the same
but do change
learn to ride them
lucky some day
you might be free
and others may call you
brilliant
talented
or sane

i

I'm up--the fever broke
like a bad joke
surrounded by silence
and Christian Science
sweats and regrets
helping hands mostly dead
and only one who's better read
inelegant quotations require devotions
like the muscle in the leg
the gray mush in your head
must be stretched and pulled
old idiotic beliefs culled
distance in this instance lit the way
misguided rites past ties family and otherwise
bumping into walls
blind ambition leading to brightly lit halls
bigger roomier stalls
finding a cage the size of a stage
hard-earned much-needed praise
among the many brave ones
who choose to play to find the greater day
for they are not honest or chronic anymore
and life's not such a miserable chore

so now you believe

the devil sits in florescent-filled meetings
details details details
of such things I am never aware
as I stare at reflections of my loss
it looks back
    terra firma
    plead I do with you now
    give me twenty more years of
    love
    art
    words
    ideas
    false starts
    naked things
    weed and daydreams
    this deal I make
let this shell of a body heal
I will write prose
with breath and blood
books that the world will wish to digest
of racism and bigotry I will always make jest
humor humor humor
will win the day
and with the help of verse
I will get the last say

the lazy despot

I'm conquering the world
one letter at a time
changing this planet this earth with
simple sinful dirty rhymes
thoughtfully rottenly
spit in the ears and in the minds
of the most noble parts of humankind
enjoin the kings queens and those who serve them things
please let them know
it's to be master I'm after
far-flung mountains I will climb
shall grab the coasts when given some time
bits morsels of energy stocked away
like good weed Guinness and bottles of wine
corks popped like gun shots will someday flow forth
and I shall seize some slow-witted tribe
the Gilligan islands a valid base
to start my master race
but I am too harried and busy
and way too damn lazy
could I get some help please?

WILLIAM SICKWITT

quiet the riot

quiet growing like seaweeds
creeping its way into me
flora and fauna give tongue
rustling whispers begun in the mixed matter
where lives the mad hatter
anchored loosely to the bottom of the black sea
floating inside with long-since drowned sunken honesty
drug back upstream lead by penury
if not for you for me for all of thee
sea the surface boiling up and down to and fro
see the waves and foam twirl and whirl
take heed listen hear Psyche's desperate plea
growth suits lasting
bespeak the quiet quest for heart's ease
never having known natural serenity
hidden in the depths of you
inside me
at long last soulfulness ripe
of that sweet lovely fruit I will have
bite after bite after bite

logic

I spent till it hurt
it didn't work
trying to force
an ill-mannered course
in letting go the desperate
all encompassing ego
seed starts to peek out to grow
self-possessed ease
measured steps over
insecurities regrets immaturities
they break up and hinder they weave
all should learn to thread the needles
stitching decorously
to politely sew
details tend your stance
so you can advance
with no holes in your clothes
or in your once holy soul

too close to call

balance is out
Yin throbbing
infections rage
slowing energies flow to but a trickle
abstractions seem deathly cold
tasting scents of formaldehyde
causing pursing lips
body coming undone
shaken in stand and sit
throwing tantrums fits
mouth poisoned from want
bacteria feasting
bringing one close to an end
Yang is strong but one without the other
won't last long
glimpsing the other side
black and white mix into grey
you three are the only reason
I care to stay

baby steps

brought down
by
desperate pleasures
fucking half-measures
dry lands
dirty hands
deserts last forever
cotton-filled
parched mouths
bent over
half-curtsies
half-bows
nourished by
eating sacred cows
living by
partially thought out Taos
yet another tentative step
pulling the plow
but that's good enough for now

shelter falling in

shelter falling in
the weights of age and growth
heavy burdens
mistrust like rust never sleeps
eats away eats away
green onus growing
care for all too tall an order
costs run ever steeper
the loss of love
nothing strikes deeper

one step at a time

waling in transit
as all do
a hermit's shroud
my sackcloth of choice
inherited inner voices
giggle and shout
what is this about
let me out
let me out

a touch

tick tick tick
goes the fatalistic itch
behind the ear
holding back

a complete future
it's chance
fear of forward movement
is no improvement

mundane mistakes made
over and over
and then again
the tick tick tick

of the spark
in the center of one's heart
needs only the chance of love, a touch
to keep beating
again again and again

no team in i

stiff like a corpse
a matter of course
impudent toward change
every last day
ever more strange
no need in finding fault
or laying blame
life is managed pain
act quickly to
dissolve absolve resolve
shame
it's wasteful and inane
standing
man to mirror
mirror to man
have a plan
measured in
heart-gripped hand

exhausted

tiny steps
inching us
towards the edge
dual holy oath
more an organic pledge
ended by a vision
of dread
lifting the future
the light
at the end
of the tunnel
green

steady boy

losing the grip
feeling it slip
a foremost hold
growing tired old
tentative it was
grasp long held
beliefs turned to ash
kept draining away
from the skin
lest one be not rash
haste is a short erratic space
the slow girl said
heed her warning
she's pretty smart and plus
she's better read

90 | WILLIAM SICKWITT

sordid way

heartsease wash over me
to breathe is not to be
the blind can see
shades of darkness
of gray light
grasping at other's wishes
seamless dreams
my only
crooked
ways and means

deserved be the scorn
of me
unequal treatment shelled out
the past come round about
unfair without a doubt
conscience suffering
from gout
wine
hash
too much stout
stepping out
smoking out
messed up kind of clout
I spout
but I can't help but selfishly think
if I can't have my sordid way
I'm out

disappointment

trust crumbles like cake
into dust
understandable
unforgivable lust
human
poker-faced style protection
the feverish infections
step about take time for reflections
puddles of meter reflect
me not you
hard to do
see beyond you
for gone factors
neo sky's mud pies
Nobel size dreams
mad schemes
cake goes back to sort of flour
bide the hour
the art is fine
patience dear lad
give serendipity her time

lungs burn fire
harps words and wishes
striving blindly
blowing for something
her
hair falling in colored strands
blow to find love
build the pyre
light it with
hot air
lust
loneliness
death and desire

play mother fucker play

WILLIAM SICKWITT

a box

is a poem mother wrote after William's death

May I please have a box, sir
a box for my son's ashes?

He got too tired of fighting
against the fear anguish addiction pain
the excruciating loneliness.

Can I get it slightly bigger? I need room for
pieces of my heart, his brother's dad's sister's too.

We all loved Star Wars you know,
the dark side against the force
we like to think the demons left for the dark side but
all the smiles joy hugs laughing hazel eyes love
and good melted into the force

Oh, thank you, sir
that box is just right.
It leaves enough room for all he desired
calm hope serenity
the peace he now has.

biography

Born August 16, 1968 in Arcadia, California, William Joseph Lanier's life was a struggle before it had begun. Born nine weeks early, he spent his first 28 days under constant watch in a neonatal intensive care ward. On September 12th, having won the fight to live, he was brought home and greeted by his older brother Steve, age 3. William would have his own opportunity to welcome a sibling when his little sister, Michele, joined the family 15 months later.

The family moved to Texas in May of 1970, settling in the small North Dallas town of Little Elm. William immediately proved different than other children of his age when he began attending primary school. When tested, he exhibited an extensive vocabulary with word comprehension levels more common among children 2 to 3 years older than himself. Like many naturally brilliant children, though, he struggled through his secondary education. In the early seventies, learning disabilities like ADD and ADHD had not been officially recognized; they were a stigma to be covered, not an ailment to be treated. Later in life, when reflecting upon his early education, William often commented that he could never maintain focus.

His struggles eventually caused his parents to enroll the troubled youth in a boarding school in Albuquerque, New Mexico, for his ninth grade year. His behavior spiraled further out of control, and William came to the realization that the school structure wasn't for him. He left the institution behind, and although he did not graduate from high school, did eventually attain his G.E.D.

A friend introduced William to drugs at a very young age. This dalliance with substance abuse would lead to a lifetime of addiction, characterized by constant battles to keep himself clean.

Despite his struggles with education, drugs and ADHD, William forced himself to stay productive and worked in the food industry in his early years after high school. While excellent for gaining work experience and practical training, the positions he was holding had no promise of promotion, nor the benefits or pay to sustain him. William took the initiative and applied for a hotel food service job in the Cayman Islands. He worked there for one year, but with no real progression to his career path turned instead in a different direction and joined the Army National Guard in 1991. After graduating from basic training, he transferred to Fort Sam Houston in San Antonio, Texas, to train as a medic. He was proud to serve his country.

He took a break to help his mother and step-father build their passive solar home in Palo Duro Canyon near Amarillo, Texas. He spent the next six months helping to sculpt the landscape, build and mud walls all in an effort to help construct his parents' dream home. Beyond the simple pleasures of helping one's parents, though, his time in construction led to an unforeseen product; his first poem, Snow.

In 1994, William began a new thrust at gainful employment, and became a Massage Therapist eventually gaining employment at the Grand Spa in Addison, Texas. He enjoyed the position so much that he stayed at the location for 12 years, and was considered not only a veteran of the craft but one of the most valued employees at the spa.

For 4 years, William had been a brother, son and remarkable employee, but in March of 1998 he added a new role to his life; uncle. His sister Michele and her husband Clark welcomed their daughter, Elizabeth, into the world on the 29th of March. "Betz" and William fell instantly in love. He took his responsibility as uncle seriously, and was extremely active in her life. He babysat, participated in or attended her sporting events and was always keen for another adventure.

When Betz was learning to speak, she gave William a nickname that stuck. She loved apples and she loved her Uncle Bill. She combined the two loves and created the nickname "AppleBoo." The poems Apple Who and Loved by One, At Least were inspired by her. They shared a passion for music and arts, and he often would play the blues harp for her.

In 2004 he met the woman who would become his wife. They shared a passion and love for dogs, and became the proud parents of Megan, a Golden Retriever, and Loki, a Malamute. Both dogs developed health issues, and while William and his wife went to great expense providing the hip surgeries necessary to improve Loki's quality of life, there was no amount of money which could cure Megan's cancer. Megan's death inspired the poem Boob. After Megan's passing, they adopted another Golden, Luna. William and his wife divorced in 2010, and he was devastated when his ex-wife severed all contact between himself and his dogs.

After his divorce, William decided to move to Austin. He had been actively writing under the pen name William Sickwitt for some time and decided that Austin was the right atmosphere to cultivate his talent, determined as he was to make a name for himself in the writers' scene. He instantly earned a job at Massage Envy to help pay for rent and groceries while he wrote, and also began volunteering at Austin Pets Alive animal shelter (APA). He loved the animals so much that he ended up taking a second job at APA.

He became a regular on the poetry scene, often taking the stage on open mic nights, instantly making many friends that would form a close group of individuals who shared his same passions. He was living his dream of an authentic "bohemian" lifestyle, and gave every appearance of happiness. He often commented to his family in Dallas about how much people enjoyed his harp playing and poetry.

Poetry was not, however, a sustainable practice for William. The buildup of debts coupled with the expense of living in Austin proved too much for him. He battled depression periodically throughout his life, and debt combined with his loneliness pushed him to a state of hopelessness.

On August 13, 2012, William took his own life. His body was discovered three days prior to his 44th birthday. Everyone who knew him was shocked and grief-stricken by his choice, but the family vowed to honor his last request, written in a final letter to them. He asked that they publish his writings.

The family has done their best to hold true to his vision of An Awful Lot. He chose the cover image and the title. They only wish he had stayed and published this book the exact way he had imagined it. The following quote was found in his possession upon his death:

"All men dream: but not equally. Those who dream by night in the dusty recesses of their minds wake up in the day to find it was vanity, but the dreamers of the day are dangerous men, for they may act their dreams with open eyes, to make it possible."

-T.E. Lawrence, Seven Pillars of Wisdom: A Triumph

Profits from the sale of this book will be donated to various charities including, but not limited to Austin Pets Alive - www.austinpetsalive.org, The American Foundation for Suicide Prevention – www.afsp.org and Suicide Survivors – www.suicide.org.

www.ingramcontent.com/pod-product-compliance
Lightning Source LLC
Chambersburg PA
CBHW042008150426
43195CB00002B/60